STORYMAZE

6

THE OBELISK OF EEENO

written and illustrated by

TERRY DENTON

ALLEN & UNWIN

FOR ANN JAMES

First published in 2003

Allen & Unwin
83 Alexander St
Crows Nest NSW 2065
Australia
Phone: (61 2) 8425 0100
Fax: (61 2) 9906 2218
Email: info@allenandunwin.com
Web: www.allenandunwin.com
Visit Terry's website at: www.terrydenton.com

The National Library of Australia
Cataloguing-in-Publication

Denton, Terry, 1950 –.
The Obelisk of Eeeno.

For children.
ISBN 1 74114 089 7.

I. Title. (Series: Denton, Terry, 1950– Storymaze; 6).

A823.3

Cover and text design by Terry Denton and Sandra Nobes
Set in Helvetica by Sandra Nobes
Printed in Australia by McPherson's Printing Group, Maryborough, Victoria

10 9 8 7 6 5 4 3 2 1

1

OOOPS!!
You took me by surprise.

I have just had my new brain fitted. You are human so you probably don't have this problem. My brain grew too big for my old head. Unfortunately the head-fitters couldn't find a new head of the right size.

Well, they did find *one*, but it was really ugly. Made me look just like a human being and I couldn't live with that!

So, instead of finding me a new head to accommodate my bigger brain, they found me a new brain to fit my old head. Makes sense.

And it's a beauty too. This new brain belonged to an illustrator, so it's hardly ever been used. And some really interesting stuff has been left behind inside. And a lot of rubbish too. Anyway, I'm having fun exploring it all. There are lots of old memories and smells and sights and sounds.

Only problem is that when the head-fitters downloaded the stuff from my old brain into the new one, there wasn't enough room for everything. So now there are lots of things I can't recall. I don't remember my phone number, or how to get home, or how many legs I have.

But the headfitters say it's only temporary. They are getting me a second smaller brain to take the overflow, but it hasn't arrived yet. I will have to keep it in a bowl in my office.

Unfortunately, this story was in my old brain, and I just fed that to the dog. So I don't know what's going to happen next. It will be a surprise for both of us.

Anyway, let's get on with it.

2

Claudia shakes Nico awake from his dream.

'Nico. Nico, wake up, nappy-breath,' she says.

'What?' says Nico.

'It's time to go.'

'**NO!** How could you wake me, Claudia? I was just about to hold up the trophy.'

'Well, if we don't go now, *Prince Charming*, you'll never get your hands on that trophy.'

'Go?' says Nico. 'Go where?'

'Wake up, needle-brain! Don't you remember anything?'

Mikey, who has been standing next to Claudia, patiently explains.

Today is THE day!

Nico, Claudia and Mikey are leaving Ithaca and travelling to distant Ganymede for Nico's latest attempt to win the World Surfing Championship. And this time he is an absolute certainty to win. His main rival, the five-times previous winner, Hercules, has been sent on a mission to the Underworld to bring back Cerberus, the three-headed dog. Big task! He'll never be back in time.

'Have you seen M.I.T.?' asks Mikey.

'No,' says Claudia.

'No,' says Nico.

'He's been a bit strange lately,' says Mikey.

'Maybe his voice is breaking,' says Nico.

3

There's something you should know about space/time travel devices like M.I.T. – they can be very temperamental. M.I.T. is no exception. He takes the Ithacans to wrong destinations so often, he has them convinced that he is faulty.

Maybe he really is.

There was the time Nico, Claudia and Mikey wanted to visit Murillion. He took them there all right, but two million years earlier than they wanted. They ended up knee-deep in blue-green algae fighting off prehistoric mosquitoes.

Have you ever been attacked by a prehistoric mosquito? Dangerous creature! A Narrator friend of mine was attacked by one just last year. It held him in its foul arms and sucked him dry. Blood, bones, organs, credit card, the lot! All gone. We scared the beast away, but too late, poor William was a mess. Just like a sausage skin without the sausage. His wife was very upset. She is a very practical woman, so she had him stuffed and propped him up in the living room to scare off robbers.

But that's another story!

'Where is that little microbe?' asks Claudia.

'Look! Over there on the beach,' says Mikey, pointing to M.I.T., who is sitting on the sand chatting to a headless doll.

M.I.T. is in love. And, although it is hard to tell what a headless girlfriend might be thinking, she may well be in love, too.

'I hate to break up this little love affair,' announces Claudia, grabbing M.I.T. 'But you have work to do.'

'101100.' M.I.T. is unhappy about leaving his girlfriend, but he is programmed to obey. Besides, Claudia is dragging him away by the arm.

'110001,' yells M.I.T. Then turning to his girlfriend he calls out, '01110.'

PLIK!

M.I.T. delivers the Ithacans to the World Surfing Championships on Eastern Ganymede. He is very angry at being so rudely snatched away, so to punish his owners he has brought them to a parallel universe called Edemynag. It seems perfectly normal, but just a few things work in reverse. **Like the surf!**

Nico is not surprised that the surf is backwards. He just thinks that's the way things are on the east coast of Ganymede. He has no idea he is being tricked, and that he is really on Edemynag.

The waves are a bit scary. They are thirty metres high and move faster than any other waves in the universe. Apart from soundwaves. And light rays. And really fast rocket-propelled stingrays. But Nico doesn't mind. He's surfed monster waves before – and survived.

Nico works quickly to master the art of surfing backwards. A wave suddenly rises up at the water's edge and Nico jumps on from the beach and rides it out to sea. It is just like a film of giant Hawaiian waves on Earth played backwards.

Nico surfs brilliantly as usual and by the last heat, he has a huge lead on the scoreboard, 6:3, 7:6, 5:1 and 40:0. Ooops! Sorry! That's the tennis score from the French Open. I can't find the surf score. Anyway, on Edemynag the scoring system is much too hard even for me to follow. So just take my word for it: Nico is a certainty to win the competition.

Claudia gives him some calming advice.

'Don't do anything stupid, monkey-brains!'

Nico would surf through molten lava to get his hands on the World Surfing Championship trophy. Lucky for him, it's not that kind of parallel universe.

Nico tries a triple reverse backhand lob with high backspin torque cut-off on well-rolled marzipan icing…backwards!!! Those of you who are not surfers will have no idea what that is. But take the word of an expert, it's not easy to pull off.

Nico nails it. He sees visions of the trophy with his name already engraved on it.

Meanwhile, coming a hopeless last in this competition is a surfer called Yekim. You might know him from the other STORYMAZE books as Backwards Mikey. He is clearly the worst surfer in the universe. He can never quite make it off the beach. A couple of times he falls off in the shallows and almost drowns. And once he even lands head-first in a garbage bin on the beach, squashing a dozen seagulls.

THIS IS A <u>REVERSE</u> WORLD. SO IT MAKES SENSE THAT THE <u>WORST</u> SURFER SHOULD WIN. AND THAT IS BACKWARDS MIKEY.

5

'Oh well, that's it for another year,' says Claudia.
'Let's go home.'

'What?' yells Nico. 'Go home? No way!'

'But it's all over.'

'Oh, no it's not.'

Nico grabs hold of M.I.T.

'He's taking me to next year's World
Championship on EEENO.'

'Now?' asks Claudia.

'Now!'

Mikey convinces Claudia that one more World
Championship is not too great a sacrifice to make
for a friend.

'OK, but that's it,' she says. 'If he blows this
one, we go straight home.'

They hold hands and form images in their
heads of planet EEENO. They start to fade away.

But M.I.T. is still missing his girlfriend, who is
waiting for him on the beach on Ithaca. Not that
she has much choice. She is just an old plastic
doll propped against the sea wall. She's not going
anywhere. Besides she doesn't have a head!

M.I.T. is desperate to get back to her. But he
must obey his owners.

More or less!

'01111.'

PLIK!

'Welcome to this year's World Surfing Championships, on beautiful planet EEENO,' a loudspeaker announces loudly.

'Thank you, M.I.T.,' says Nico. 'We're here and on time!'

Not that Nico cares what year it is, as long as his name is on the trophy.

What Nico doesn't know won't hurt him. But I thought you'd like to know that M.I.T. wanted to dump the Ithacans on planet EEENO in the year 2650. That would *really* have annoyed them. But unfortunately he missed by a big margin and brought them to EEENO at exactly the right time. Which for him was the wrong time! Now he is even angrier.

NICO SURFS WELL AND BY THE LAST HEAT HE IS LEADING THE COMPETITION.

NICO, THIS TITLE IS YOURS.

YOU JUST NEED TO NAIL THIS RIDE.

18

Nico crashes into a tall stone pillar that
suddenly appears in the surf. He slides down the
side of the stone pillar and staggers along the
reef. Then he collapses on the sand. Guess who's
NOT going to be the World Surfing Champion?

The officials rush over to Nico and drag him
out of the water to safety. A doctor arrives and
starts to render first aid.

'Stand back everyone,' the officials shout. 'Let
the first-aid blokes attend to him.'

Claudia, Mikey and M.I.T. are worried about
their friend. Mikey looks across to the stone pillar
standing in the surf.

'Where did that obelisk come from?' he
wonders.

7

Obelisk?

Anyone know what an obelisk is?

I didn't either, until I looked it up in my *Narrators' Complete Guide to the Universe and Beyond*.

An obelisk is a tall pillar, usually square at the base, getting thinner towards the top and ending in a small pyramid.

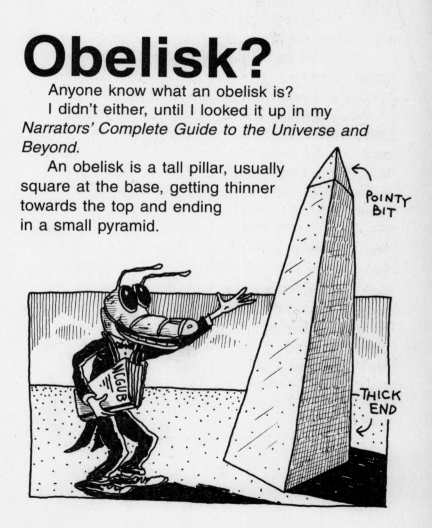

POINTY BIT

THICK END

Most cultures throughout the universe have made obelisks. The Egyptians made lots of them and believed they had mysterious powers. It was something to do with their shape.

Obelisks first started appearing on planet EEENO in the 7th century, but not because anyone on EEENO was building them. No, Space Sewers were to blame.

Do you know about Space Sewers?

They are like invisible pipes criss-crossing the universe, allowing stuff to be instantly transported across huge distances of space and time. Very few people know where and when these Space Sewers are going to appear. But there is something about the shape of obelisks that means they are always disappearing into Space Sewers. This beach on EEENO has a permanent Space Sewer outfall. It is always tipping unwanted space junk into the water. It is very dangerous, as Nico has just found out. The EEENOians in this area have been campaigning for years to have the outfall blocked up, but the government has done nothing about it. What's new?

8

Nico splutters and coughs and eventually wakes up.

'What happened?' he asks.

'You hit an obelisk,' says the paramedic.

'Fantastic,' says Nico. 'Could I order a lime spider, Muriel?'

'Claudia, he's OK,' says Mikey.

But Claudia is walking away from the first-aid blokes towards the sea.

'An obelisk?' she says, looking towards the stone pillar standing erect and tall in the water.

Is she drawn to the obelisk by the mysterious light surrounding it? Or is she seduced by the cosmic music wafting out of the rock pillar?

No, not really.

She just thinks it's unusual that a great hunk of rock has suddenly appeared in the middle of a surf beach, knocking her friend senseless.

She walks to the water's edge and out along a partly submerged rocky reef, right up to the obelisk. She examines it carefully.

The obelisk has figures carved into it. Heiroglyphiccy figures. Is that a word, heiroglyphiccy? I can't remember. I wish I hadn't thrown my old brain to that stupid dog!

Heiroglyphiccy? Maybe it wasn't a word, but it is now!

Claudia's nose is almost touching the obelisk now, and she runs her fingers over the carved figures.

'Oh, my god!' she says, as if she has just stepped out of an American sit-com. 'That looks just like Minotaur.'

If you don't know who Minotaur is, you should read *The Minotaur's Maze,* Book 5 in the **STORYMAZE** series. But I can fill you in.

If I must!

Minotaur was Claudia's boyfriend. Well, *she* thought he was her boyfriend. Minotaur was not so sure. But because Claudia fell in love with him, she decided to rescue him from his prison in a maze on Knossus. It was all a bit of a disaster really because he didn't want to be rescued. Anyway, they made wings and flew out of the maze. But Minotaur's wings fell apart when he soared too high and he plummeted into the ocean and disappeared, presumed drowned. And he was never seen again…until now when his image has turned up on this obelisk in far off EEENO.

'I don't get it,' Claudia says. 'Why would Minotaur's image be on this obelisk?'

'Good question,' says Mikey, who has joined her on the reef. 'Maybe it is some monument to him from his family.'

'Why did it appear here? Now?'

'Look at what you're standing on,' says Mikey.

'Holy Occhilupo!' says Claudia.

The reef is not a natural reef at all. It is made up of thousands, maybe millions, of obelisks dumped here by the Space Sewers. Some are quite new. Some old. Some so old they are crumbling to dust. They are just like monuments in a graveyard.

'Why Minotaur?' wonders Claudia. 'What does it mean?'

'I don't know,' says Mikey. 'I guess it could be some kind of sign.'

'Of what?'

'I don't know,' says Mikey. 'But Minotaur's family might know something about it.'

Claudia thinks about this for a while.

'Maybe we should go to Knossus and ask them,' says Claudia.

'Minotaur's father might still be angry with you, Claudia. After all, you took his son away.'

'That's true. But he might get over it if there's a chance I can bring his son back again.'

'What about Ariadne?'

9

Do you know Ariadne?

She is the daughter of King Minos who runs the health farm on Knossus. She is Minotaur's brother and she's a bit loony. She has spent most of her life trying to get rid of her brother. So she wouldn't be very happy if Minotaur reappeared again.

And no one is saying he will reappear. But Claudia certainly thinks it is a possibility...maybe.

You must remember that all of this started with a carving of Minotaur on an obelisk on EEENO. And who knows what that means?

Actually, I do!

That's because we Narrators know everything.

Anyway, back to Claudia who has been thinking things over.

'Mikey! I need to know if Minotaur is alive or dead. We'll have to go to Knossus,' announces Claudia. 'His family are my only lead.'

'OK, Claudia,' says Mikey. 'I guess that makes sense. Count me in.'

'Where're my chips and lime spider, Muriel?' asks Nico.

He is slowly recovering from his sudden obelisking.

Claudia holds up M.I.T. 'Let's hope this genetically engineered lemon can take us there.'

'10001.'

Claudia, Mikey and the slightly deranged Nico huddle around and lay their hands on M.I.T.

'To the King Minos Health Farm on Knossus,' Claudia whispers. And slowly they all fade away.

Forever maybe?

Not forever.

The Ithacans reassemble just next to a sign pointing to the health farm. Claudia and Mikey set off to find King Minos and Ariadne.

'You go ahead,' says Nico. 'I need to chill. I'll take M.I.T. for a walk along the beach.'

'Cool,' says Mikey. 'We'll pick you up when we're finished.'

Nico is not letting on to the others, but now that he is feeling OK, he is desperate to get back to the World Surfing Championships on EEENO. He doesn't want to go near the health farm because Ariadne might see him. She has the hots for Nico and he is scared of her.

So Nico and M.I.T. wander along the beach skimming stones and picking up shells. But not just shells. This beach is covered with all sorts of plastic junk from all over the planet – plastic cups, drinking-straws, bottles and toys.

11

While that little soap opera takes place, Claudia and Mikey arrive at the health farm.

'We'd like to see Ariadne,' Claudia says to the assistant at the front desk. The assistant shows them into the manager's office.

'Wait here,' she says. 'The manager will be with you shortly.'

The walls of the big office are covered with framed certificates and pictures of King Minos and Ariadne posing with some of their more famous clients. But there are no photos of Minotaur.

Suddenly the door opens and Claudia and Mikey brace themselves for a blast from King Minos. But Ariadne walks in.

'Mikey. Claudia. How good to see you,' says Ariadne.

Claudia notices her badge. In big letters it says

Manager.

'When did you take over from your father?' asks Claudia, pointing to the badge.

'Oh! So you haven't heard,' says Ariadne. 'My father died some months back. Some say he died of a broken heart. I guess he never got over losing Minotaur.'

'That's terrible,' says Claudia.

'So now I run the place on my own,' says Ariadne. 'But what brings you here?'

'Minotaur,' says Claudia.

'Oh, him,' says Ariadne, grinding her teeth.

Claudia tells Ariadne the story of Nico's collision with the obelisk of EEENO.

'Poor Nico,' says Ariadne. 'Is he OK? Take me to him!'

'He'll mend,' says Mikey.

'The important thing is that the obelisk has carvings on it,' Claudia continues. 'And when I looked at them closely, guess what?'

'You've got me!' answers Ariadne.

'Minotaur!' announces Claudia. 'The carvings are of Minotaur.'

'So?' says Ariadne.

'Did you have an obelisk made with Minotaur's likeness on it?'

'No! Why would we do that?' snaps Ariadne. 'Father never wanted anyone to see Minotaur, alive or dead.'

'Oh,' says Claudia. 'We didn't think of that. So you know nothing about the obelisk?'

'It's a mystery to me,' says Ariadne.

'I reckon it's a sign that Minotaur might still be alive,' says Claudia, looking hopeful.

'Still alive!!' screeches Ariadne.

'Well, I don't know for sure,' says Claudia. 'But maybe he didn't drown when he fell out of the sky.'

'He might have been sucked down into the Underworld,' suggests Mikey. 'He could be trying to contact us. Or trying to escape.'

'So Minotaur might not be dead,' says Ariadne. Then she thinks, *He might start wondering why his wings fell apart so easily on that fateful day.*

'But how could he not be dead, Claudia?' asks Ariadne. And she thinks, *He might have realised someone sewed stones into his clothes to make him sink quickly.*

'Ariadne, I touched that obelisk,' says Claudia. 'And I had this really strong feeling he was with me somehow.'

Ariadne smiles at Claudia, but she frowns on the inside. And she thinks, *I will have to watch Claudia. I don't want my brother coming back into my life now that the health resort is mine at last.*

But the obelisk has her tricked. She knows nothing about obelisks.

'You say it suddenly appeared in the sea,' Ariadne asks. 'Maybe that is the clue.'

'The sea?'

'My father had an old friend who knows much about the secrets of the seas,' says Ariadne. 'He may be able to help us.'

'Can we talk to this bloke?' asks Claudia.

'Difficult. Old Nick is on the other side of the planet on one of his fishing expeditions.'

'No problem,' says Claudia. 'M.I.T. will take us there.'

12

PLIK!

M.I.T. lands Nico, Claudia, Mikey and Ariadne on Old Nick's boat. In fact, he's quite pleased with himself, because he lands the Ithacans and Ariadne knee-deep in dead fish in the hold at the bottom of the boat. Unfortunately the fishing boat is out in the middle of the ocean at the height of a wild, wild storm. Old Nick is battling to keep his boat afloat.

Not a good time to drop in!

'You flathead!' hisses Claudia, throwing a fish at M.I.T.

'You did that on porpoise!' says Mikey.

'He must have a haddock!' says Nico, who has completely recovered from his close encounter with the obelisk.

The travellers scramble up on deck brushing off bits of fish. Mikey finds a dead octopus in his pocket. They stagger to the wheelhouse.

'Nice perfume,' says Old Nick. He is holding the wheel and desperately trying to keep his boat pointed in the direction of the wind and waves.

The sudden appearance of four-and-a-half helpers might be unsettling to you or me, but Old Nick doesn't even bat an eye-patch. He has, after all, sailed through the Rocks of Doom in the Great Sea of the Underworld. You'd never get me to go there for all the tea in Ionia Vitaldehyde 247 Nebula Beta-Alpha Centoriiii.

'Welcome aboard, my little sardines,' he yells, glad of the extra hands. 'Don't just stand there, you two. Man the bilges!'

'Bilges?' asks Mikey.

'Shiver me timbers!' says Old Nick, scratching his wooden leg. 'Don't they teach you kids nothing?'

He looks at Mikey and Nico and points down stairs in the direction of the hand bilge pump.

'We're filling with water, you barnacle-bums,' he croaks. 'Start pumping!'

Nico and Mikey rush off.

Meanwhile, Old Nick directs Claudia to tie down all the loose equipment in the wheelhouse.

While he concentrates on keeping the boat on course, Ariadne monitors the weather radar.

'So, lass, what's new?' asks Old Nick. 'And more to the point, how's me favourite ol' rascal Minotaur?'

'Favourite old rascal, eh?' seethes Ariadne quietly. 'Always Minotaur, isn't it?'

'Still got the young beast locked up, have you?'

'Not really,' replies Ariadne. 'He escaped a while back. I thought you knew.'

'Maybe I did,' says Old Nick. 'But that was then and this is now. And it must have fell out of me head.'

So Ariadne tells him the long story of Minotaur and his mysterious disappearance, of the sad death of her father and of the sudden appearance of the obelisk of EEENO.

'AAAARRRHH!!!' says Old Nick. 'King Minos gone. And poor Minotaur!' Old Nick falls silent for a few moments, then he pipes up again. 'So, lass, Minotaur's likeness on an obelisk, eh? That is mysterious.'

'That's what we thought,' says Claudia.

'This sounds like the work of that slimy old sea-dog Poseidon.'

'Who's Poseidon?' asks Claudia.

'You've never heard of Poseidon, lassie? He's only the all-powerful Greek god of the sea.'

Just then a huge wave crashes over the boat and floods the engine, which gives a few coughs and then falls silent. Old Nick calls Nico and Mikey back up from below deck.

'Hold on to this wheel, lard-bucket,' he says, handing the wheel to Mikey. 'And you stay here,' he says pointing to Nico. 'In case something happens to him.'

'You girls come with me,' says Old Nick, giving them a lantern and a bag of tools to carry.

He hurries out of the wheelhouse and heads towards the engine.

Nick starts tinkering with the motor, letting fly with a few sailor curses.

'Poseidon is not in the best of moods today, as you can see. He can be quick to anger. Obviously something's got his nose out of joint.'

Another huge wave crashes over the boat and Old Nick drops his spanner, which slides across the deck. Claudia dives rugby-style and catches it. She hands it back to the captain.

'Good catch, lass.' He coughs a few times then continues. 'Poseidon is a grumpy old fart. It's mainly jealousy. People keep mixing him up with King Neptune, who is the ROMAN god of the sea. No one has a clue who Poseidon is, but they all know good old King Neptune. And that annoys the heck out of Poseidon.'

'Sounds like you know him well,' says Claudia.

'Oh, yes,' says Old Nick. 'We've had our moments.'

Old Nick kicks the engine, and utters a few more choice curses. Then he gives up and they all rush back to the wheelhouse.

'Here's my guess,' says Old Nick. 'That ol' rascal Minotaur wandered into Poseidon's undersea world and did something to anger him. If you make Poseidon angry enough, he might well turn you to stone. Or trap you in an obelisk. It happened once to a friend of a friend of a friend of mine.'

Meanwhile, the storm suddenly gets even wilder. Waves crash over the boat and it lurches violently to one side. Then the stern begins to dip and the pointy bit lifts up.

'We're done for, lass,' says Old Nick, as another huge wave crashes on deck. 'Me boat's goin' down. Leave now by whatever magic you came. Escape while you still can!'

'Come with us,' pleads Ariadne.

'No, lass! I've got a date with old Poseidon!'

There is an almighty shudder as another wave crashes over the boat. M.I.T. is washed away from his friends towards the edge of the boat. Nico desperately reaches out for him.

A HUGE WAVE CRASHES OVER THE BOAT AND M.I.T. IS WASHED INTO THE SEA.

41

44

Nico, Claudia, Mikey and Ariadne fight for their lives as the huge seas roar and crash all around them.

Nico struggles towards Claudia. A monster-wave thumps him from behind. It pushes him under the water. He stays under for almost a full minute. When he resurfaces, he smashes his head against something hard.

'OUCH! What the...?'

Nico instinctively clings to whatever it is.

It is a plastic bathtub!

Judging by the smell and the green bath ring, it is from Old Nick's boat and hasn't been washed for decades. He probably cleaned his fish in it. Still, even a fishy floating bathtub in the middle of a stormy ocean is not to be sniffed at.

'Over here!' Nico calls to his friends. They all clamber into the bathtub. They struggle to keep the tub upright against the force of the raging sea. The battle is long and difficult. Most battles are! All night they take turns baling out water with their bare hands as they totter on the brink of life and death.

Will they survive?

How about you decide.

I'll give you a choice. Turn to **Chapter 15**, page 47, and ride out a violent storm with our heroes.

Or...

Advance to **Chapter 16**, page 52, and take your chances.

It's up to you!

15

Nico, Claudia, Mikey and Ariadne lie asleep in the bathtub. It is morning and the sea is calm. On the huge expanse of the ocean, there is nothing to be seen except for one tiny bathtub drifting with the current. There is no sign of M.I.T.

The gentle current has carried them a great distance across the sea.

Mikey wakes first and looks around.

'What's up?' asks Claudia, sleepily.

'Not much,' says Mikey. 'It looks like a fog is rolling in.'

'Where did the world go?' asks Nico. The mist has descended over their bathtub. They can see nothing and they can hear even less.

Our heroes have disappeared down a plughole in the ocean. You'll have to jump ahead a few pages to **Chapter 17**, page 60, to catch up with them.

16

Welcome, brave reader, from **Chapter 14**.

Nico, Claudia, Mikey and Ariadne have been paddling and baling furiously all night. Around dawn, the storm finally calms down. Our heroes slump exhausted in their bathtub and finally they fall asleep.

A seagull lands on the edge of the bathtub. It looks down at the sleeping figures.

'Wake up!' screeches the seagull. **'Time to wake up!'**

Mikey wakes first and looks up at the seagull.
'What?' he says.

Now Claudia, Nico and Ariadne are all awake
and looking at the seagull.

'You heard,' says the seagull. 'Shake a leg. It's
time to meet the Great One.'

'Who are you?' says Mikey.

'I am just an ordinary seagull,' says the
seagull. 'My name is Jonathan. I am a messenger
from the Great One. He wishes to meet you.'

'Who is this Great One?' asks Mikey.

'I think he means Poseidon,' Claudia suggests.

'No time for a discussion,' says Jonathan. 'You
can stay out here in the middle of the ocean and
starve to death if you wish. Or you can come and
meet my master. The choice is yours.'

'Who is your master?' Mikey asks.

'The Great One,' says Jonathan.

'Who is the Great One?' Mikey asks.

'My Master,' says Jonathan.

'This is getting us nowhere,' growls Claudia.
'I'm tired and cold and hungry. And I've had
enough. Take us to your leader.'

'OK, sailor.'

Jonathan whistles. Which surprises me
because I didn't know seagulls could whistle. See,
I bet you didn't think you would learn something
like that today! Nor did I. Books like this
are so educational!

Anyway a few seconds after Jonathan's whistle, a pod of dolphins arrives. They nudge the bathtub to turn it around. With a couple of dolphins up the front steering, the rest push from behind and the bathtub moves surprisingly quickly across the ocean.

The Ithacans have no idea where they are being taken and they are too tired to care.

'These dolphins look very angry,' says Nico.

He's right. They are a pod of parallel universe evil killer dolphins. They are the Great One's secret agents.

The prisoners, for that is what they have become, fall back into a gentle sleep.

'Wake up!' screams Jonathan. 'We're here.'

The prisoners look out of their bathtub. The dolphins have brought them to a tropical island. There is a sign that reads: 'Welcome to the Island of Square.' And when Nico, Claudia, Mikey and Ariadne look about, they see that the trees are square and the houses are square. In fact, everything is just a little bit squarer than usual. Even them.

A big square penguin marches up to the
prisoners.

'The Great One is expecting you. Follow me,'
says the penguin.

'Have a great time,' says Jonathan waving to
them. The big penguin blows a whistle and a
squad of square penguins marches up.

'To the Great One,' the big penguin orders.

The squad surrounds our friends and they all
march off up the hill.

'Cute penguins!' says Nico. 'Where are you
taking us?'

'QUIET!!' yells one of the penguins, snapping at Nico with vicious teeth and nearly biting his nose off.

The prisoners are brought to the top of a hill where they stop before a great gleaming goldfish.

Nico looks at Mikey. 'We can understand him!'

Indeed they can. M.I.T. is talking in a very clear, but slightly mechanical, tone. They can understand every word he says. They will soon wish they couldn't.

'You, brainless ones!' says M.I.T. 'You may wonder why I have brought you here before my wonderfulness.'

He pauses.

'You are here for justice. Your crimes are many. But fear not. You will not be put on trial now for your evil deeds against the Great One. That is not how we do things on Square Island.'

The prisoners breathe a sigh of relief.

'Here on Square Island we always punish you first, then we put you on trial.'

Now M.I.T. looks directly at Claudia.

'You, the tall lizard one! Your crimes against my magnificence are the greatest. So you will be punished first.'

Next the Great One reaches into the air and suddenly sprinkles dugong dust in Claudia's eyes.

At first nothing happens, then slowly Claudia fades away.

And if you want to find out what happens next, you will have to slowly fade away too.
Go to **Chapter 18**, page 64.

Quick, off you go, or you might miss something!

17

Welcome from **Chapter 15**. You are just in time. The story is starting.

Nico, Claudia, Mikey and Ariadne wake out of what seems like a dream. They are lying in a bathtub deep down on the floor of the ocean.

'Am I still breathing?' asks Mikey.

'Am I still alive?' asks Nico.

'We seem to be,' says Mikey.

'That's amazing!' says Nico.

'You're amazing!' says Ariadne, moving closer to Nico.

They look around at the group of buildings that surround them. They are carved from coral, in the many varied and brilliant colours that coral can be.

This series of buildings of unimaginable beauty is Poseidon's undersea palace. But do our heroes care? No, the barbarians! They are only concerned with discovering a way back to the surface.

'We must find M.I.T.,' announces Claudia.

They cross a courtyard and wander down a street between two rows of coral buildings. The soft coral waves in the gentle deep-sea current.

'I still don't get this,' says Nico. In fact they are all still confused at being able to walk and talk and breathe even though they are at the bottom of the ocean.

'Who do you think lives here?' asks Nico.

'This is Poseidon's Palace,' says a strange voice.

Nico turns around to find two tridents pointing at him. (A trident is a spear with three points instead of one point. A trident makes three holes in you instead of one. Three times as much blood means you die much quicker.) Attached to each trident is a guard.

'There is no escape,' says one of the guards.

'What if they have guns, Gordon?' says the other guard.

'Guns will not work underwater, Derek!' says Gordon.

'They might have Cerberus, the terrifying three-headed dog. Then they could escape, Gordon.'

INSIDE THE FISH, M.I.T. STRUGGLES TO ESCAPE.

'Do you see a terrifying three-headed dog, Derek?'

'Well, no, Gordon, I don't.'

'So there is NO escape!!!'

'They might have a dehydrated three-headed dog, Gordon.'

'Do you see a...? STOP THIS, DEREK! There is no escape.'

The Ithacans and Ariadne are surrounded by the two guards. Which is difficult to do.

'We must take them to Poseidon, Gordon,' says Derek.

'I know that, Derek.'

'Well, I was just saying...'

'Do you always have to state the bleeding obvious, Derek?'

'Yes, Gordon,' says Derek, stating the bleeding obvious.

OK, dear reader, to find out what happens to our underwater friends, you will either have to wait till the movie comes out, or turn ahead a few pages to **Chapter 19**, page 67.

18

Welcome, dear readers from **Chapter 16**.

Claudia has faded away and reappeared in a hyper-modern world somewhere in a parallel universe created by the Great One.

A woman stands outside a house. Inside, a beautiful prince lies sleeping. He has been asleep for one hundred years.

One hundred years! His toenails must be about three metres long by now. His beard big enough to cover an entire suburb! But the woman is not thinking about that. She is just thinking about breaking into the house.

She sneaks up to the door and turns the handle. It opens. She steps inside. In front of her is a staircase. She steps towards it. **CLICK!** A huge hammer swings down and pulverises her. A laser gun blasts and she vaporises. All except for her skull which falls into a pile of other skulls on the hallway floor.

Meanwhile, outside, another handsome young woman approaches the house. This is Claudia. She runs at the door and kicks it down. Matrix-like, she pivots in the air and the pulverising hammer swings harmlessly past. Claudia runs up the staircase to the handsome prince's bedroom. The lasers fire, but Claudia is too quick. She whips out her make-up mirror and shines it at the lasers.

'Fry, you lasers,' she purrs.

They explode. She continues on, kicking the door down. Claudia leans over the sleeping prince. He is the most handsome man she has ever seen. With just one kiss she knows she will wake him and they will fall in love and live happily ever after.

Claudia smiles.

'This is a dream come true.'

She puckers up and kisses the handsome prince. But the instant her lips touch his face, it swells up into two large spotty cheeks that look just like Nico's bum.

In fact it is Nico's bum. And Claudia is kissing it. **'OOOOHHH, YUKKK!!!'** she screams. 'That's disgusting!'

Suddenly Claudia vanishes.

Instantly she reappears outside the house. She remembers nothing of what just happened. The Great One has erased her memory.

Claudia runs at the door and kicks it down. Matrix-like, she pivots in the air and the pulverising hammer swings past harmlessly. Claudia runs up the staircase to the handsome prince's bedroom.

And so on and on and on forever!

'MMMAAAWWW HHHAAAWWW HHHAAAWWW!'

The Great One, M.I.T. laughs.

To avoid endless repeats of this chapter you must move on. Turn to **Chapter 20**, page 70.

19

Hello.

We're all in jail here. You should have stayed in **Chapter 17**, it was much better there.

Deep down in the dungeons of Poseidon's undersea palace, Mikey sits cold and alone leaning on the bars of his prison cell. He was dragged away to the dungeons on his own, so he has no idea where his friends are. Or how he is going to get out.

'Where is M.I.T. when you need him?' thinks Mikey. 'Without him, we might never escape.'

And then Mikey's thoughts turn to his beloved home on Ithaca. A famous old Ithacan folk song comes to his mind.

You know the one. Everybody knows it. Although I seem to have forgotten it for the moment. It was in my old brain which is soon to become a pile of dog poo in my back garden.

But you must know the tune! It's just on the tip of my tongue.

In times of trouble, it always makes Mikey feel better to hum this old Ithacan folk tune. So he starts humming.

In a cell not too far away, Nico wakes from a fitful half-sleep. He hears Mikey's humming and recognises the tune. Nico starts humming too.

Soon Claudia hears the song and joins in.

'Are you all in a cell together?' Ariadne asks. By now the Ithacans are singing at the tops of their voices.

'No,' they all call back from different directions.

'SILENCE!' yells the jailer.

But now they know they are all OK and close together.

'AAAARRRHHH, me hearties!' yells another familiar voice.

'Old Nick!' calls Ariadne.

'SILENCE!!' yells the jailer. 'Or I'll cut your tongues out and…'

'Let me guess,' says Nico. 'You'll feed them to the dogs.'

'Yes,' says the jailer. 'The dogs are hungry and we're fresh out of entrails.'

Later that night, when the jailer is snoring soundly, the prisoners feel free to talk.

'You know much about Poseidon?' Old Nick asks.

'No!' says Nico.

'He rides around on a chariot pulled by golden seahorses. And he carries a mighty trident that he uses to stir the seas up, causing huge and violent storms. He rules the waves with the help of the

Cyclopses. These giant one-eyed beasts do all his dirty work.'

'Yeah, well, everybody knows that!' says Ariadne.

'Well, what you don't know is that Poseidon is under investigation by Zeus's God Squad. They suspect him of organised crime.'

'Who is Zeus?' asks Nico.

'Zeus, my little monkey, is Poseidon's brother. He is also the most fearsome king of all the gods.'

To find out more about Zeus and Poseidon and all that, turn to **Chapter 21**, page 76.

POSEIDON.

20

Congratulations, you escaped from **Chapter 18**. You are back on the Island of Square. The Great One is addressing Mikey.

'For crimes against the Great One...' he announces. But M.I.T. doesn't bother finishing the sentence. He just reaches up into the air and sprinkles dugong dust in Mikey's eyes.

At first nothing happens. Then slowly Mikey begins to fade away.

?
THAT LOOKS LIKE A GIANT CREAM BUN.
SOME HOURS LATER MIKEY KNEELS BEFORE THE BUN.

Mikey lies on the sand, his lips throbbing with pain. He looks up to the horizon. In the distance he can just make out a shape. It looks like a bowl of custard.

'I'm so hungry,' says Mikey, crawling towards the bowl of custard.

When he gets a bit closer he looks up at it again. He realises that it is not just an ordinary bowl of custard.

'It is a bowl of lumpy custard. I love LUMPY CUSTARD.'

Mikey crawls as quickly as his tired, hungry body will allow. In a few short hours, the poor ragged-kneed boy stands before a giant bowl piled high with lumpy custard.

He tries to resist.

'So many calories!' he tells himself. 'But I am so very, very hungry.'

With his last tiny particle of strength he climbs up the side of the bowl. He stands on the edge for a moment, then he dives into the lumpy custard with his mouth wide open.

'Come to me, lovely custard!' he cries.

But, as he plunges in slow motion towards the lumpy custard, it transforms into a bowl of writhing, festering, slimy maggots.

'AAARRRGGGHHH!!!' Mikey cries.

SPLATTT!!!

Mikey rises out of the bowl of writhing, festering, slimy maggots.

He turns around and looks with disgust at the writhing, festering, slimy maggots that surround him.

'I am so very, very, very hungry,' he sobs.

Then he looks at us watching him.

Mikey looks back at the maggots again.

'Eh! What the heck!' he says.

He picks up a spoon and starts eating.

Meanwhile back on the Island of Square, the Great One stands before Nico.

'Monkey-headed Nico,' says M.I.T. 'At some time in the future you will betray me. **Betray the Great One!** Unforgivable! Prepare for your punishment!

The great one sprinkles dugong dust in Nico's eyes.

'Your punishment,' he says, 'is to go back to **Chapter 15** and work your way through this whole story.'

And for you, dear reader, the punishment is exactly the same. You must all go back to **Chapter 15**, page 47.

NOW!!!

21

Welcome from **Chapter 19** to this powerful and moving **Chapter 21**. Possibly the most important in the book! It is brought to you by our sponsor, the Haggis Burger Corporation, sellers of the finest Haggis Burgers in the universe!!!

'A Haggis Burger a day, keeps the zits away!'

The next morning, Poseidon summons the prisoners to his court for interrogation. He walks back and forth for some time, looking at them very carefully. Finally he speaks.

'Who are you?' he asks. 'And what are you doing here?'

Claudia steps forward.

'We were lost at sea,' she says. 'We thought we had drowned. But now we are not so sure.'

'Not sure, eh?' says Poseidon. 'Well, I am sure. I am sure you are spies! Just like the other one.'

'The other one?' asks Claudia.

'The evil spy of Zeus!'

'This evil one,' says Claudia. 'Was he called Minotaur?'

'Don't speak his evil name in my presence!' yells Poseidon.

'Has Minotaur been here?' asks Ariadne.

'Aha, that spy! That scoundrel. That evil plotter! He descends into my watery world...but goes straight to Hades who takes him to meet that high and mighty brother of mine, Zeus...Zeus thinks I am a criminal and sends the spy back down here. Undercover!...Zeus offers him immortality and a seat with the gods in heaven... All he has to do is get some dirt on me...help Zeus destroy Poseidon's power forever...'

Poseidon continues, showering his prisoners with litres of saliva as he rants and raves.

'...Zeus, of all people, my bitter enemy...so this Minotaur turns up down here...*BAAAH, I said his name again!*...and takes a job in the palace...

eavesdropping…reporting back to Zeus…telling lies, lies, lies…but my Cyclopses sniff him out and discover he is up to no good…'

Poseidon hardly draws a breath as he continues his story.

'…he is a slippery one that Minotaur…*BAAAH, I said his name again*…he pokes out the eye of one of my dim-witted Cyclopses and escapes… and **takes my trident with him**…

MY FAVOURITE TRIDENT!!! Can you believe it?…he

tries to run off to Zeus, but we capture him and shut him up in a big stone obelisk…and shove him into a Space Sewer…and the sewer sucks him away and spits him out somewhere on the other side of the universe…and he's never seen again…

'But he has **MY FAVOURITE TRIDENT!**

'…stupid fool Cyclopses locked the trident in the obelisk with him…**MY BEST TRIDENT!** So I sent them away…

'"Don't come back without it," I said to the Cyclopses. "Or I'll feed your entrails to the Gorgons."

'…and I'll do it too…don't you think I won't… Zeus will be laughing his head off at this…and me, Poseidon, armed with only my spare trident...creating storms and tsunamis that are barely ripples!'

As Poseidon rages, Claudia realises that she knows something Poseidon doesn't.

She knows where the obelisk is. And she remembers that the carving on the obelisk shows Minotaur holding a trident in his hand.

So maybe Minotaur has the trident with him, she thinks.

Claudia is right! Poseidon's trident is locked up in the obelisk with Minotaur.

But what she doesn't know is that the obelisk of EEENO could be on the move at any moment. It might suddenly disappear up the Space Sewer and reappear somewhere else in the universe. It happens to my socks all the time.

Then again it might not. The beach on EEENO is covered in obelisks that went nowhere!

Randomly appearing obelisks are very unpredictable.

22

'Excuse me, your wateryness,' says Claudia, risking Poseidon's wrath. 'I think I know where your trident is.'

Poseidon stops, mid-rave.

'My trident?' he says. 'My very best trident?'

Claudia nods.

'Where?' asks Poseidon.

'I'm not going to tell you…yet.'

'What?' thunders

Poseidon. 'I'll have you fried in oil and…'

'Feed her entrails to the dogs?' suggests Nico.

'Yes,' says Poseidon, delighted.

'Entrails to dogs!'

'If you want your trident back, you will have to do something for me,' Claudia continues. 'You will have to tell me how to release Minotaur…'

'BAAAH! Don't say that name!'

'You will have to tell me how to release him from that obelisk. In return, I will get your trident back.'

'I will destroy you rather than do a deal with a mere mortal,' Poseidon screams, waving his second-best trident about, blowing up a few minor storms and wiping out a few island civilisations somewhere in the universe.

'Guards!'

While Poseidon is busy summoning his guards, Nico absentmindedly takes the doll's head out of his pocket. The precious doll's head he is carrying back for M.I.T., the doll's head he promised to guard with his life.

He puts it on his finger, like a puppet.

And while Poseidon angrily rants on and threatens his prisoners with tortures and punishments too numerous to mention, Nico plays with the head.

'Poor little Mikey, your entrails are as good as dog's meat,' says Nico, wobbling the head of the doll and throwing his voice as if it is the doll that is talking.

'Quiet,' Mikey whispers to Nico. 'You'll only make things worse.'

'How could things possibly be worse?' replies the doll's head.

'Good point,' says Mikey. 'Anyway, no one could ever be fooled by your pathetic attempt at ventriloquism.'

23

Well, almost no one.

In the middle of his ranting, Poseidon happens to glimpse the talking doll's head.

Suddenly he falls quiet.

Despite his vast experience of things in the godly realm, Poseidon has never seen ventriloquism before.

What a wasted life!

He is totally sucked in by the nodding doll's head.

'Ariel!' he whispers in shock. 'Speak to me, Ariel.'

Poseidon believes that the doll's head is Ariel. Not Aerial, the thing on your car. And not that other Aeriel, the ancient god of radio waves, or whatever. But the other, other Ariel, who is the hero of that Disney mermaid film. It is Poseidon's favourite movie. And he thinks Ariel is the greatest movie star in the universe.

He doesn't know she is a simple drawing on a bit of plastic. And I'm not going to be the one to tell him.

It is just a short step then for Nico to grasp that Poseidon is so much under Ariel's spell he will do anything she tells him.

'Poseidon, great god of the sea,' says Ariel.

'Oh, my hero speaks to me!' gasps Poseidon. 'What do you want?'

'I am here to help you.'

'How, my sugar-plum fish?'

'Do you wish to get your favourite trident back?'

'Indeed I do, my little sea-star.'

'Then tell the tall ugly one how to release Minotaur from his obelisk.'

'I will do this, my little sea-cucumber.'

'And in return, she will promise to throw your trident back into the sea.'

'Brilliant plan, my coral trout.'

'But be warned, oh Great Wet One, all of this will come to pass only if the tall ugly one kisses the handsome one called Nico…now.'

'Consider it done, my beautiful little butterfish.'

Poseidon turns to Claudia. 'You heard Ariel. If you want me to tell you the secret of the obelisk, you must first kiss Nico.'

'No way!' shouts Claudia.

'I will happily do this task instead of you,' says Ariadne, stepping forward.

'No, it must be Claudia,' insists Ariel. 'And it must be on the lips!'

'On the lips,' repeats Poseidon.

Claudia is seething with anger as she approaches Nico with her lips poised, but she dare not upset the irrational Poseidon.

'You realise you will die for this,' she whispers to Nico.

'Eh! It's worth it,' he whispers back.

And Claudia kisses Nico. Just a quick kiss on the lips. But not as quick as you might imagine a quick kiss on the lips would be. Claudia's lips linger longer than they should for a really quick kiss. Does this mean she extended the kiss because she was actually enjoying it? Or were her lips simply stuck momentarily to Nico's sticky chewing-gum lips? We will never know.

84

'OK,' says Claudia. 'What is the secret of the obelisk of EEENO?'

'Can I trust you?' asks Poseidon. 'How do I know you won't just release your friend and steal my trident?'

Old Nick steps forward and stands before Poseidon.

'What if one of us stays behind as a hostage?' he asks.

'A hostage?'

'Yes,' says Old Nick. 'The hostage stays 'ere while them others goes back to EEENO. When you gets your precious trident back, you releases the hostage. Simple!'

'Poseidon would accept that,' says Poseidon. 'Which one of you will be my hostage?'

'Me,' says Old Nick. 'I will stay behind as a hostage.'

'I won't let you do that, Nick,' says Ariadne.

'You won't allow it, lass? Since when does the daughter of Minos tell Old Nick what to do?'

Poseidon stands up, pointing his trident at his prisoners.

'I accept this smelly old sea dog as a hostage. The rest of you go! I am sick of the sight of you.'

Then Poseidon lowers his voice to a menacing whisper.

'But if you dare to double-cross me, I will hunt you to the ends of the universe.'

'Quick,' says Mikey. 'Let's go before he changes his mind.'

Nico starts to leave with the doll's head still on his finger.

'Ariel, my little sausage skin, you must stay with me, too,' says Poseidon. 'We have much to talk about.'

'Well, Great Wet One, of course I will stay with you,' Ariel tells him. 'But first, let my friends depart. And then I will need my beauty sleep. Wake me in three hours.'

Mikey coughs and holds up four fingers.

'No, make that four hours,' says Ariel.

When they last see Poseidon, he is walking down the watery corridor with Ariel's head, ready to tuck her into bed.

'Good riddance, you pack of ratbags,' calls Old Nick.

'Farewell, Nick,' Ariadne calls back. 'We'll get you out of here, quick-smart.'

'Don't hurry, lass,' he replies, holding up a pack of cards. 'I might play a bit of poker with Poseidon. After a few hands with these cards, this place will be all mine.'

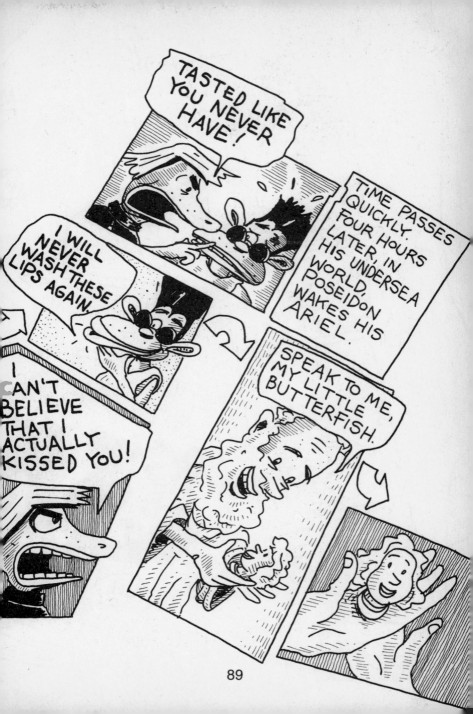

89

PLIK!

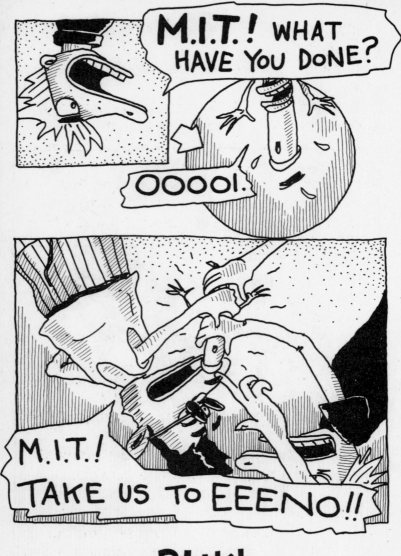

PLIK!

Claudia looks around. The world is right side up this time.

'That's better, M.I.T.!' she says. 'I don't know why you couldn't do that the first time!'

Claudia quickly strides off along the beach towards the obelisk of EEENO.

Mikey, Nico and M.I.T. follow, singing that famous old Ithacan folk song and thinking of home. Ariadne is straggling further behind. When she sees Claudia getting close to the obelisk, she hurries to catch up.

Mikey laughs. 'You should have been there M.I.T. Nico pulled the coolest ventriloquism trick on Poseidon.'

'And he fell for it,' laughs Nico. 'Did you see his face?'

'Just brilliant, Nico,' says Mikey. 'Where did you get that stupid plastic doll's head from?'

'It was in my pocket...' Nico says, then glances down at M.I.T.

'Well, that was a lucky break,' says Mikey. 'Do you always carry an old doll's head in your pocket?'

M.I.T. looks up at Nico.

'Shouldn't we be trying to release Minotaur from the obelisk?' says Nico, desperately trying to change the subject.

'111100.'

M.I.T. explodes with rage. He realises that Nico gave away **his** girlfriend's new head in return for their freedom. The very head he promised to guard with his life.

'10001.'

'But I didn't have any choice, M.I.T.,' pleads Nico.

IIIOII.

Meanwhile Ariadne joins Claudia on the reef in front of the obelisk of EEENO.

'Poseidon told me how to release someone from an obelisk,' says Claudia. 'It takes just one kiss from someone who loves the person locked inside it.'

Claudia reaches out to kiss the carved Minotaur on its carved lips.

'Stop, Claudia!' shouts Ariadne. 'I think it is a trick.'

'What?' says Claudia, through her almost-kissing lips.

'I think **Poseidon** is trying to double-cross **us**!'

'What?' say Nico and Mikey, who have just joined Claudia and Ariadne on the reef. 'Why would he do that?'

'What if he had his favourite trident with him all along?' argues Ariadne. 'What if he made up the whole trident story so we would come here and be trapped in the obelisk with Minotaur?'

'Claudia is the only one kissing the obelisk,' says Nico. 'The rest of us will be okay.'

'But I won't be okay!' says Claudia. 'Anyway, what makes you think he still has his favourite trident?'

'That storm he threw at us,' says Ariadne. 'It was a beauty. His spare trident could never do that! He said so himself.'

'Why would he want to imprison us?' asks Claudia.

'I don't know,' says Ariadne. 'He's a loony! That might explain it.'

'But I've got to kiss the obelisk or Minotaur will be trapped in it forever.'

'Oh, well,' says Ariadne. 'It's your choice, Claudia.'

'And what about Old Nick?' asks Claudia. 'We can't abandon him. Who knows what Poseidon will do to him.'

If they only knew what I know.

At this very moment, Old Nick is playing strip poker with Poseidon. And poor old Poseidon has lost everything. His clothes, his shoes, his undies, his spare trident, his complete collection of Greek god tazos. The only things he still owns are his undersea palace and Ariel. And they are now playing double or nothing for the palace.

Poseidon can't believe his bad luck. But what he doesn't know is that Old Nick is playing with specially marked cards that he got from an old pirate a couple of years back. Poseidon doesn't stand a chance. And it's not much use him getting angry because he doesn't have his trident any more. So he can't turn Old Nick into a frog. Or an obelisk.

But that's another story.

26

Claudia stands before the obelisk of EEENO, pursing her lips and pondering her predicament.

With just one kiss, she can rescue Minotaur, the love of her life, from the obelisk. On the other hand, that one kiss might imprison her forever in the obelisk, and she's not sure she wants to spend forever locked up in a stone pillar with Minotaur.

Forever is a long time. Even with her precious Minotaur.

'Wait, Claudia!' says Nico, rushing forward to be by her side. 'Don't do anything you might regret.'

'What?' says Claudia. 'Like kissing you!'

As Nico nears Claudia, he trips on a bit of rock.

He loses his footing on the slippery reef.

He falls forward.

He tries to stop himself falling.

He fails.

He falls.

He crashes into Claudia.

She falls forward.

She tries to stop herself crashing into the obelisk.

She fails.

She falls onto the obelisk.

Her lips are still pursed.

Those still-pursed lips hit the obelisk first.

In fairytales, kisses have amazing power. They can turn grown men into frogs. And frogs into grown men. You might think that Claudia's lips crashing into the obelisk doesn't count as a real kiss. But in the world of magic spells, this lip-smack is a legally binding kiss.

Instantly the obelisk of EEENO trembles.

'Ouch!!' yells Claudia. 'My bleeding lips!!'
The obelisk starts to crack and splinter.

'Can't you watch where you are going, Nico, you block-head?'

The obelisk crumbles to dust before their eyes. Minotaur steps forward from the obelisk and collapses into Claudia's arms.

'My hero,' he sighs and then they kiss.

'She's got rocks in her head,' mutters Nico.

'And in her hands,' sighs Mikey.

'#%@!!!&#!' hisses Ariadne. Her secret plans for disposing of her brother forever are thwarted, temporarily. To ease her frustration she moves a bit closer to Nico.

27

Nico needs to be daring. He decides to try a move he has been practising back on Ithaca. It's next to impossible, but if he can nail it, he will get the points he needs to overtake Hercules.

'This wave!' Nico says. He paddles furiously and is swept up by the wave.

'OK,' he shouts. 'Who dares wins!'

He tries a double underhand-grommet, sunny-side-up with wink-toggle and fries on the side. And if you have never surfed before, you would have no idea what that is. I have no idea what that is!

Nor how difficult it is. But true surfers know it as the second most difficult of all surf moves. Apart from getting your wetsuit on and off that is!

Does he succeed? Well, don't look at me! How would I know?

The answer to that question is in a steaming pile on my back lawn.

28

Meanwhile back at the beach on EEENO.

Claudia and Minotaur stand arm in arm watching Nico attempt the impossible.

'Claudia,' Minotaur says.

'Yes, my love!' says Claudia.

'I have decided something.'

'What?'

'I am not going to take the trident back to Poseidon. I am taking it to Zeus.'

'What?'

'Without his trident, Poseidon's power will be destroyed. His days of crime and violence will be over forever. And Zeus will be so pleased with me. He will richly reward me.'

Ariadne overhears this conversation. She smiles. This is the opening she has been waiting for. She moves closer to her brother.

'But, Mini, Poseidon warned us not to double-cross him,' says Ariadne.

'But, Ari, this is what Zeus would want,' says Minotaur.

'And what about Old Nick?' asks Claudia. 'What will happen to him?'

'This is BIG, Claudia,' says Minotaur. 'More important than some washed-up old fisherman.'

Poseidon snatches his spare trident from under the card table and raises it above his head and in an instant, storm clouds gather over EEENO.

THWACK!

There is a crack of thunder and a bolt of lightning hits the beach where Minotaur is standing. The sea erupts with a big, twister-cyclone-tsunami.

Although I must tell you, I have seen bigger storms! You can tell Poseidon is using his spare trident. But it is a big enough storm to suck the surfers up into the sky and then scatter them all over the beach.

29

When the sand settles and the sea calms down, there are two obelisks standing in the surf and two giant Cyclopses hurry back into the water, carrying Poseidon's favourite trident.

Mikey and Nico rush across to the obelisks. Mikey stands up next to the taller one, touching its side.

'Poor Claudia,' says Mikey. 'She's trapped inside.'

'I don't think so,' says Claudia, wandering up behind Mikey and Nico.

'You're here!' says Nico. 'So who's in the obelisks?'

'Ariadne and Minotaur would be my guess,' says Claudia. 'I stepped away at just the right time.'

'Maybe we could leave them both in there,' suggests Nico.

At that moment, a strange rumbling, squishing, sewery kind of noise starts up.

'What's that?' asks Claudia.

Mikey points to the two obelisks, which are trembling.

'The Space Sewers!' he yells. 'The obelisks are about to be sucked back into them. Do something. Quickly!'

'My Minotaur,' yells Claudia sprinting across the reef to the obelisks.

Unfortunately she trips on the same bit of rock that Nico tripped on earlier. And she slips on the same slippery reef he slipped on.

I won't bore you with the frame-by-frame replay. But you know what's going to happen.

Luckily Claudia remembers to pucker up her lips as she falls. She crashes into one of the obelisks and is knocked out cold. But the impact of her puckered lips counts as a kiss, just as it did a couple of chapters ago. One of the two obelisks instantly crumbles to dust.

Unfortunately, the other unkissed obelisk doesn't do any crumbling. Instead, it is sucked up into the Space Sewer and instantly disappears.

30

A wave crashes over the unconscious Claudia and she starts to shake herself awake. She looks up at the out-of-focus figure standing over her.

She hopes that she has kissed the right obelisk and saved Minotaur from an eternity trapped inside a pile of rock.

Another wave crashes over Claudia and she looks up again through watery eyes at the figure above her. She cannot make out who it is.

'Ariadne!' Claudia moans. 'It's you, isn't it?

OH, NNNNOOOOO!! I kissed the wrong obelisk!!'

Claudia slumps down on the reef again, screaming, 'Ariadne, you evil beast! You made me destroy my Minotaur!'

Nico and Mikey lift Claudia up and carry her to the shore.

'It's OK, Claudia,' Mikey says. 'Minotaur is here. He is OK.'

'Minotaur is OK?' asks Claudia. 'And Ariadne?'

'She was in the other obelisk when the Space Sewer took it,' says Mikey. 'Who knows where she is now?'

'Oh, poor Ariadne!' says Claudia.

31

The last heat of the World Surfing Championship is about to start…**again.**

Claudia, Minotaur and Mikey stand on the beach watching their friend Nico battling with Hercules.

Nico waits in the water for that perfect wave. He rejects heaps of waves that Hercules catches. But for poor old Herc, none of them produce that winning ride.

And then Nico sees it. The ten-out-of-ten wave. He paddles like a mad dog and feels that brilliant rush as the wave snaps him up.

He unwinds the double underhand-grommet, sunny-side-up with wink-toggle and fries on the side. It might well be the most difficult move attempted in the whole history of the universe, more or less. It's a bit like you trying to stay upright.

'Brilliant,' says Mikey.

'This could be it,' says Claudia. 'Nico's moment.'

'Just like it could have been my moment,' says Minotaur. 'I could have destroyed Poseidon!'

'What?' says Claudia.

'Stupid Poseidon!' says Minotaur. 'He had no idea I was working undercover.'

'Quiet, bean-brain. He might hear you.'

'Poseidon is so dumb!' shouts Minotaur. 'King Neptune would never have fallen for that.'

Mikey and Claudia pounce on Minotaur and wrestle him to the ground. M.I.T. brings some kelp for rope and a gag. They all look up into the sky to see if there is any response from Poseidon. But although the sky is cloudy, there are no fireworks.

'That's it!' says Claudia. 'I've had enough. What are we going to do with him, Mikey?'

At that very moment, the skies clear above the beach. Claudia, Mikey and M.I.T. look up.

121

32

'Welcome back to the World Surfing Championship,' says the Master of Ceremonies.

We missed the end of the last heat. That was Zeus's fault. So we'll have to wait for the M.C.'s announcement to see who won.

Nico and Hercules stand on the podium, nervously waiting for the result. Nico thinks he has done enough to win, but he's not sure. Whereas Hercules *is* sure. He can't even imagine defeat.

'Ladies and Gentlemen and others,' shouts the M.C. 'I won't keep you in suspense any longer!'

But he does. He has a list of several million people to thank, right down to the plankton that feed the microbes that feed the crabs that clean the beach. Eventually he runs out of people to thank and comes to the important announcement.

'This year's World Surfing Champion is...the one and only...'

He fumbles with the envelope.

'...Nico of Ithaca!'

Claudia, and Mikey and M.I.T. rush onto the podium and swamp the stunned Nico.

Hercules can't believe it.

'But I'm a superhero. I've never lost anything in

my life,' he wails. He shuffles from the podium, a crushed man. Slowly he stumbles off towards the Psychological Counselling tent.

Meanwhile Nico is carried around on his friends' shoulders, pumping his fists in the air and throwing kisses to the crowd.

'Do you have anything to say to the people out there?' asks the M.C.

'Yes,' says Nico. 'This is the greatest moment of my life.'

Then he shouts in triumph, 'I love youse all!'

'Nico, what does this win mean to you?' yells the M.C. over the crowd noise.

'It's a pay-off for all my hard work and all the support from my friends,' says Nico, looking at Claudia and Mikey. 'And now maybe it will allow me to get ahead. To do even greater things.'

M.I.T. looks up suddenly. He is stuck on the second last statement. *To get ahead?*

To get ahead!!

'I got a head once,' M.I.T. thinks. '**But Nico gave it away!**'

M.I.T. quietly seethes. He will have his revenge.

'11111,' he whispers.

M.I.T. begins quietly humming that famous old Ithacan folk tune. You know the one. Everybody knows it. It's on the tip of your tongue. It's that song that brings a tear to the eyes of all true Ithacans.

M.I.T. hums louder and the eyes of Nico, Claudia and Mikey fill with tears, and their minds flood with heart-warming images of home. The beach. The sky. The beach boxes. The rolling hills. Their favourite Haggis Burger store.

Together they stand on the podium, holding hands and singing that old Ithacan folk tune at the tops of their voices.

The Master of Ceremonies steps forward to present the gleaming World Surfing Championship Trophy. He thrusts the silverware towards Nico.

But Nico's mind is somewhere else.

And now his body is about to join it.

M.I.T. smiles an evil smile.

They all begin to fade away...

33

OOOO
OOO!!!!'

Nico screams as he realises what is happening.

But it is too late!

PLIK!

As the Master of Ceremonies pushes the trophy towards Nico's waiting hands, his waiting hands disappear!

Nico disappears.

They all disappear.

M.I.T. has had his revenge!

34
A BEACH ON ITHACA.
WHY, YOU LITTLE... JUST WAIT TILL I GET MY HANDS ON YOU...
101001.

While Nico's fingers hurt, something hurts him even more. Poor Nico howls long into the night over his lost World Surfing Championship. And further down the beach, M.I.T. hugs his headless girlfriend and howls in anger at Nico for giving away the precious doll's head.

Meanwhile, Claudia stands at the other end of the beach, thinking about the one who got away. She looks up to the dark night sky and amongst all the millions of stars there is one that stands out much, much brighter than all the rest.

You should ask yourself, could this brilliant star in the Taurus constellation be Claudia's Minotaur? Did Zeus really lift Minotaur up into the realm of the gods and turn him into the brightest star of all? Will generations gaze at him in wonder for the rest of eternity?

Actually, no!

Zeus may be a powerful god, but he is too insecure to allow anyone to shine brighter than himself.

No, that most brilliant of stars that Claudia is looking at is no star at all. It is the new orbiting Haggis Burger Satellite Restaurant. It is shining especially bright tonight. And now Mikey's tummy starts to rumble.

GET OFF MY FINGER, YOU IDIOT CRAB!!!

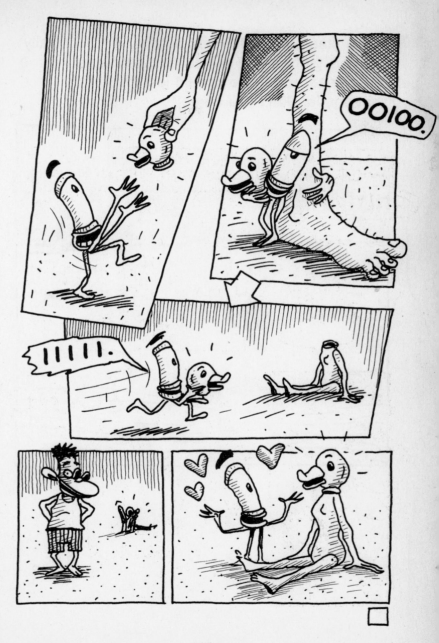

35

At this stage, I should point out that if M.I.T. really loves his girlfriend, it shouldn't matter whether she has a head or not. He should just love her for what she is. Don't you agree?

36

OK! That's it.
Clear off.

I have to go back to programming my new brain.

And you must have some homework to do. Or someone in your family to annoy.

So just close the book gently and don't bend my feelers like you did last time. It took almost a month to straighten them out again. And that's an Ionian month. Which would be a lifetime to you. Which is about how long your homework is going to take you.

Ha, ha.

And if this book has taught you anything, it should be the wisdom of the words of that old Ithacan folk song which I have finally remembered:

Which roughly translated means:

My duck is sick
My horse can't fly
And you deserve
A poke in the eye.

Cheers, thanks a lot.

The Last Chapter

A GUIDE TO M.I.T.'S* LANGUAGE

1	I hate surfing
0	There's lice in here!
00	I'm too young to die
01	You idiot!
10	I hate sand
11	Bummer
000	Oh, OH!
001	OH, NO!
010	Hello
011	Goodnight
100	Welcome back, goanna-head
101	Pooh!
110	Ouch!
111	ZZZZZ
0000	My yak has fleas
0001	HELP!
0010	Oh, joy
0011	Go away
0100	That's handy
0101	You double idiot
0110	Why me?
0111	And two hard-boiled eggs
1000	Hee hee
1001	This is another fine mess
1010	I'm not coming out
1011	His feet stink
1100	What about my TV?
1101	What about me?
1111	I'm outta here
00000	My head hurts
00001	It's not my fault
00011	That would hurt
00100	This is nice!
00101	This is serious!

00110	The roof is leaking
00111	Hello, ugly!
01001	Hold my hand
01010	Can't make me
01100	Not telling
01101	What's this?
01110	Bye, bye
01111	GRRRR!
10001	Die, you fiend!
10010	Get this smelly lump off me
10101	Just following orders
10111	Panic stations!
11000	Hello, strange animal-headed people
11011	Smarter than you, lizard-brains
11111	HEE HEE HEE
100000	It's only a flesh wound
100011	I want my mummy
100101	Just following orders, fly-breath
100111	Quiet, you stupid animal-headed people
101001	Can't catch me!
101010	Put me down!
101100	Let me go!
101110	What the @%£#$* am I doing here?
110001	You smell, lizard-brains!
110010	Holy Occhilupo, you're ugly
110011	Get your bottom off my leg
110101	Holy Occhilupo!
110110	Gulp!
110111	The whole world's turned dark
111001	My feet are on fire
111010	I hate water
111011	@%&#$*!!
111100	NNNOOO!
111101	The kettle's boiling
1110111	Yes!

*M.I.T. (pronounced *em-eye-tee*) is short for Mental Image Transfer.

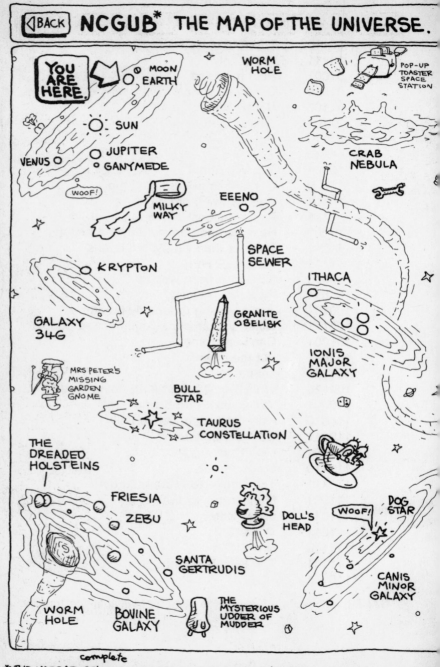

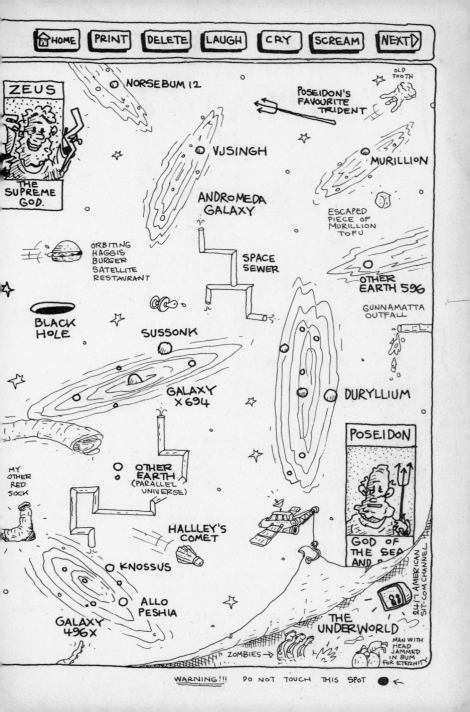

COLLECT THE
STORYMAZE
SERIES!

Look out for the next
STORYMAZE
adventure!